Meet

Ben
Franklin

with Elaine Landau

Enslow Elementary

an imprint of

Enslow Publishers, Inc.

40 Industrial Road
Box 398
Berkeley Heights, NJ 07922
USA

http://www.enslow.com

For Jeannie and Stephen Schwartz,
very special librarians, very special people

Enslow Elementary, an imprint of Enslow Publishers, Inc.

Enslow Elementary® is a registered trademark of Enslow Publishers, Inc.

Library of Congress Cataloging-in-Publication Data:

Landau, Elaine.
    Meet Ben Franklin with Elaine Landau / Elaine Landau.
        p. cm. — (Explore Colonial America with Elaine Landau)
    Includes bibliographical references and index.
    ISBN 0-7660-2555-1
    1. Franklin, Benjamin, 1706-1790—Juvenile literature. 2. Statesmen—United States—Biography—Juvenile
literature. 3. Scientists—United States—Biography—Juvenile literature. 4. Inventors—United States—Biography—
Juvenile literature. 5. Printers—United States—Biography—Juvenile literature. I. Title. II. Series.
    E302.6.F8L35 2006
    973.3'092—dc22

                    2005023185

Printed in the United States of America

10 9 8 7 6 5 4 3 2 1

To Our Readers: We have done our best to make sure all Internet Addresses in this book were active and appropriate
when we went to press. However, the author and the publisher have no control over and assume no liability for the
material available on those Internet sites or on other Web sites they may link to. Any comments or suggestions can be
sent by e-mail to comments@enslow.com or to the address on the back cover.

Illustration Credits: American Philosophical Society, pp. 18, 38 (bottom); Archive Photos/Getty Images,
pp. 39, 41; Centers for Military History, p. 35; Clipart.com, pp. 22 (bottom), 25 (top); © Corel
Corporation, pp. 37, 45; David Pavelonis, Elaine and Max illustrations on pp. 1, 3, 4, 5, 6, 7, 10, 15, 18,
21, 24, 31, 34, 37, 39, 42, 43; Elaine Landau, p. 43; Enslow Publishers, Inc., pp. 4–5 (map), 34; Hemera
Technologies, Inc., pp. 9 (top), 11; Hemera Technologies, Inc./Enslow Publishers, Inc./Library of
Congress, backgrounds on pp. 3–7, 43–48; Image courtesy The Franklin Institute Science Museum,
Philadelphia, PA www.fiu.edu, p. 29 (top); Independence National Historical Park, pp. 7, 16 (top); © The
Image Works, p. 9 (bottom); Kean Collection/Getty Images, pp. 13, 23; The Library of Congress, pp. 1, 6,
8 (top), 12, 14, 22 (top), 24, 25 (bottom), 27, 30, 32, 33, 36 (left), 38 (top), 40, 44; © Museum of
London/HIP/The Image Works, p. 20; © North Wind Picture Archives, pp. 16 (bottom), 17, 28; The
Philadelphia Contributionship for the Insurance of Houses from Loss by Fire, p. 26; Photos.com, pp. 10
(bottom), 19; Reproduced from *The American Revolution: A Picture Sourcebook*, by John Grafton, published
by Dover Publications, Inc. in 1975, p. 8 (bottom); Smithsonian Institution, p. 36 (right); © SSPL/The
Image Works, p. 29 (bottom).

Front Cover Illustrations: David Pavelonis (Elaine & Max); Hemera Technologies, Inc./Enslow
Publishers, Inc./Library of Congress (collage at top); The Library of Congress (Ben Franklin meeting
people).

Back Cover Illustrations: David Pavelonis (Elaine & Max); Hemera Technologies, Inc./Enslow Publishers,
Inc./Library of Congress (collage at top); The Library of Congress (Ben Franklin).

Contents

Ninth Street

EighthStreet

Pennsylvania Hospital

Seventh Street

Independence Hall

Sixth Street

Liberty Hall: Home of the American Philosophy Society

Fifth Street

Pine Street

Spruce Street

Philadelphia Contributionship

Walnut Street

Fourth Street

BEN FRANKLIN'S
PHILADELPHIA

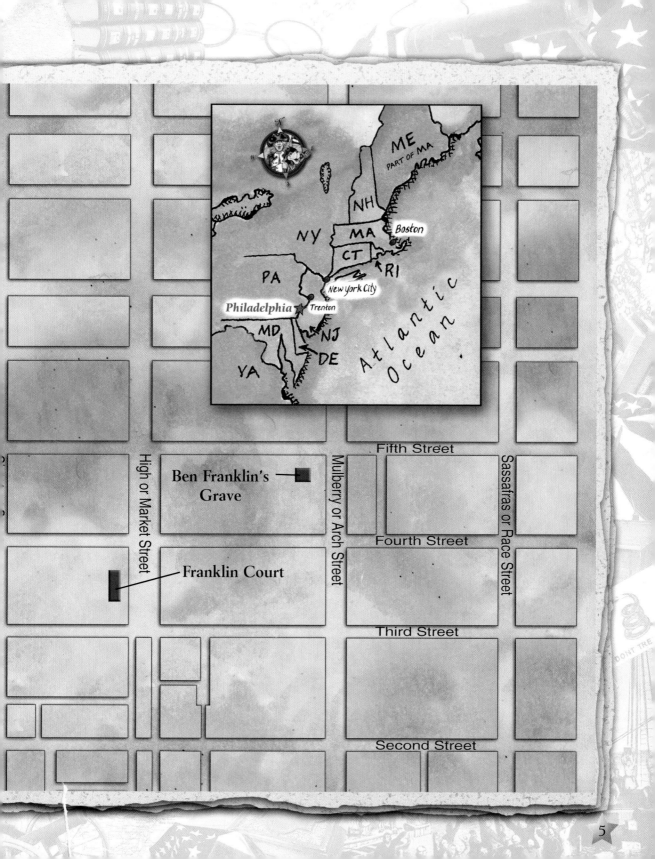

ME
PART OF MA

NH

NY

MA

CT

Boston

RI

PA

New York City

Philadelphia   Trenton

MD

NJ

DE

VA

Atlantic Ocean

Fifth Street

Ben Franklin's
Grave

Mulberry or Arch Street

Sassafras or Race Street

Fourth Street

Franklin Court

High or Market Street

Third Street

Second Street

Dear Fellow Explorer,

What if you had a time machine? Imagine using it to visit the past. Where would you go? Who would you want to meet?

I'm Elaine Landau and this is my dog, Max. Max and I do lots of time traveling. Today we are going to colonial America.

Ben Franklin

Benjamin Franklin helped write the Declaration of Independence, along with John Adams, and Thomas Jefferson.

Philadelphia was one of the most important cities in colonial America.

Max wants to see the exciting city of Philadelphia. He hopes to meet an amazing man there. This man was a successful inventor and writer. He also worked on both the Declaration of Independence and the Constitution. His name is Benjamin, or Ben, Franklin.

Why not come along with us? Use this book as your time machine. Fasten your imaginary seat belt. To begin your trip, just turn the page. Blast off!

WOW, LOOK AT ALL THOSE SHIPS IN THE HARBOR!

DURING COLONIAL TIMES, PHILADELPHIA WAS ONE OF THE COUNTRY'S GREATEST SEAPORTS.

1

It All Started on a Sunday . . .

Ben Franklin was born on January 17, 1706. It was a Sunday. His mother, Abiah Franklin, had gone to church that morning. She came home and gave birth. Then Ben's father, Josiah Franklin, took Ben to church to be **christened**. Ben Franklin would later say that he spent the first day of his life in church.

Ben Franklin was born in this house in Boston (right). Boston was a colonial port. A port is a place from which ships can come and go.

Ben Franklin was his mother's eighth child. His father had been married before. He had children from that marriage too. So Ben was his father's fifteenth child. Ben was the youngest boy in the family. That made him special to his family.

The Franklins lived in Boston, Massachusetts. Massachusetts was a British **colony** in America. Boston was a growing colonial city. When Ben was born, about six thousand people already lived there. The city had a busy harbor as well. Ben's father was a **tradesman** in Boston. Tradesmen were skilled in a particular craft or trade.

Josiah Franklin made soap and candles. These both were made from animal fat. This caused his workshop to smell bad. But he was used to the foul odor.

Ben hated making candles in his father's shop.

Ben came from a religious home. His father led the family in prayer for an hour each morning. They prayed together again in the evening.

Ben's father had wanted him to become a minister. So when Ben was eight, he went to school for that. He was soon the best student in his class. Yet, within the year, his

Ben practiced his penmanship often. He would need the skill. As an adult, he wrote a lot.

Ben dreamed of becoming a sailor, but his father would not allow it.

father took Ben out of the school.

A minister had to study for many years. Ben's father did not think that he could pay for this training. After Ben left school, he studied **penmanship** (handwriting) and math with a teacher. He also read and studied a lot on his own.

When Ben turned ten, his school days were over. In 1716, he began making soap and candles with his father. Ben did not like the work and hated the smell.

Ben's father tried to find a trade that his son would like. The two took long walks together. Ben saw bricklayers and blacksmiths at work. His father talked to Ben about other trades in the colony as well.

However, none seemed to interest young Ben. Instead, Ben dreamed of becoming a sailor. His father was against it. One of Ben's older brothers had gone off to sea and drowned. Ben's father wanted Ben to be safe.

Josiah Franklin knew that he had to find another trade for Ben. But what could his youngest son do? No one imagined how exciting Ben's future would become.

2 In the Print Shop

Ben ended up working for his older brother. James Franklin had a printing business in Boston. He put out a newspaper called the *New England Courant*. It was one of America's first newspapers.

Ben became his brother's **apprentice** in 1718. Young boys learned various trades this way. Apprentices worked for a tradesman for nine years. The boys were fed and given a room. However, they were not paid.

For a short time, Ben tried to earn money selling poems on the street.

Ben made friends in the office of the *New England Courant.*

Being in a print shop suited Ben. He worked hard and learned quickly. Ben was also a good writer and loved to read. Often, he met booksellers who gave him different books. Sometimes Ben read all night.

Ben longed to write for the newspaper. But his brother would never print anything he wrote. So Ben began writing under a different name. He pretended to be a middle-aged woman named Silence Dogood.

Ben wrote about all sorts of things as Mrs. Dogood. Sometimes he wrote about new clothing styles. Other times he wrote about people who drank too much. Ben sent Mrs. Dogood's pieces to the paper. James printed these and the public loved them.

When James learned the truth, he was very angry. In a rage, he told Ben that he would never publish anything Ben wrote again. James had never gotten along well with his brother. At times, he even beat Ben.

Nevertheless, before long, James would need his younger brother. James had to spend some time in jail for **criticizing** (speaking out against) the colony's government in his paper. Ben ran the paper while James

Ben even ran the printing press itself when he worked for his brother.

BEN HAD A VERY GOOD SENSE OF HUMOR. HE MADE THE PAPER MUCH MORE FUN TO READ.

BEN DID A GREAT JOB RUNNING HIS BROTHER'S NEWSPAPER.

was gone. He did a fine job and many people now felt the paper was funnier and better written. More people began buying it.

When James returned, he again took charge. Ben was supposed to go back to being an apprentice. This was difficult for Ben. He now knew that he could run the paper well on his own. He felt that he deserved his brother's respect

However, James was not about to change his ways. He was not grateful for Ben's help. He was still often harsh and demanding.

Ben was tired of being treated this way. He was sixteen now—old enough to be on his own. But his brother made it hard for Ben to leave. James spoke to the other Boston printers. He told them not to hire his brother.

Ben had no choice. He would have to leave Boston. He sold some of his books to get a little money. Then in October 1723, Ben boarded a boat for New York.

He could not find work as a printer there. So he went on to Philadelphia. Ben was ready to start his new life.

③ Welcome to Philadelphia

*P*hiladelphia was an ideal place for a young man like Ben Franklin. In 1723, Philadelphia was a large and exciting colonial city. At the time, Philadelphia was bigger than both Boston and New York. It was a growing center for shipping and trade. There was a lot to see and even more to do there.

In the 1700s, Philadelphia was already a bustling city. In the background is Independence Hall. To the left is Independence Hall as it looks today.

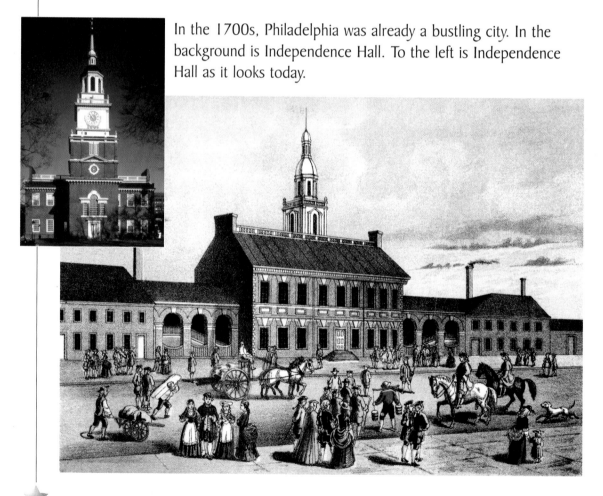

Philadelphia's busy city streets were lined with colorful houses and shops. There seemed to be people everywhere. Some sold goods while others were buying. American Indians walked the streets with animal **pelts** swung over their shoulders. They had come to the city to sell their pelts. Farmers came, too. They brought their chickens, milk, and eggs to sell.

Both entertainment and fashion were important in Philadelphia. All kinds of parties, dinners, and other outings were held. People wore stylish clothes and hairdos. They talked for hours in coffee shops and taverns.

Franklin felt at home in this exciting city at once.

Franklin was tired and his clothes wrinkled and wet when he arrived in Philadelphia.

Deborah Read Rogers took a liking to Ben Franklin right away. This portrait was painted by Benjamin Wilson around 1758.

But no one would have guessed that when he arrived. The boat trip to Philadelphia had been hard. At first the waters were choppy. The waves soaked the passengers. Later, there was no wind. Franklin and the others took turns rowing. He got off the boat looking wet, tired, and messy.

A young woman about his age noticed him walking down a city street that day. Her name was Deborah Read Rogers. Deborah laughed when she saw Ben. Dressed in his damp and wrinkled clothes, Ben Franklin was quite a sight.

At first, Ben was insulted. he did not like being laughed at. He walked away upset. Ben thought he would never

BEN FRANKLIN WAS LUCKY. ON HIS SECOND DAY IN PHILADELPHIA, HE FOUND WORK IN SAMUEL KERMER'S PRINT SHOP.

HE DIDN'T HAVE TO GO FAR TO GET TO WORK. THE PRINT SHOP WAS NEXT DOOR TO WHERE FRANKLIN RENTED A ROOM.

see Deborah again. However, he could have been more wrong.

After meeting Rogers, Franklin quickly settled in Philadelphia. He got a job working for a printer. He even rented a room from Deborah Read Rogers' parents. Ben soon forgot all about his first unpleasant meeting with Deborah. The two became quite close.

People liked Franklin. Before long, he had a number of friends. They spent many evenings talking about their favorite books. Ben looked forward to these evenings out. He enjoyed exchanging new ideas with others.

Even the Pennsylvania colony's governor, Sir William Keith, liked Ben Franklin. Keith had heard that Ben was a good printer. The governor saw that Franklin was

Franklin knew that, in order to be a good writer, he had to read a lot.

smart and hardworking. He thought that Franklin should have his own print shop. Best of all, he promised to help him get one.

4 *Off to England*

In 1724, Governor Keith said he would set Ben Franklin up in business. He wanted Franklin to go to England (part of Great Britain) to buy equipment for the shop. Franklin was to pick up letters of introduction from the governor. These would introduce Franklin to the English merchants. They would also state that the governor would pay for everything.

London was a thriving city in the 1700s. Ships brought goods there from all around the world.

Franklin went to the governor's office to pick up the letters. But the governor was always too busy to see him. He was later told that the letters would be on the ship to England.

Franklin was on the ship when it sailed. Sadly, the letters were not. Governor Keith often made such promises. He wanted people to like him. Yet being governor did not mean that he was rich. He did not have money to help Ben start a new printing business.

Franklin landed in England without much money. He went to work for a printer there. Yet Franklin still enjoyed himself abroad. He made friends and went to plays. He also loved swimming in England's Thames River.

Over the next eighteen months, Franklin worked hard. He saved enough money for his return trip home. On July 23, 1726, Franklin boarded a ship for Philadelphia. He returned without the printing equipment he had hoped to get in England.

After returning, Franklin had several jobs. Yet he still longed for his own print shop. So in 1728, Franklin went into business with a friend. His friend's father was to

THAT BEN FRANKLIN SURE LOVED TO SWIM.

HE LIKED IT SO MUCH THAT HE THOUGHT ABOUT OPENING A SWIMMING SCHOOL IN ENGLAND.

July 10, 1776.　　　　　　　　　　　　　　Numb. 2481.

The PENNSYLVANIA GAZETTE.

Containing the Freſheſt Ad-　　　　　vices, Foreign and Domeſtic.

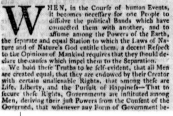

In CONGRESS, July 4. 1776.

A DECLARATION

By the REPRESENTATIVES of the UNITED STATES of AMERICA, in General Congress assembled.

WHEN, in the Courſe of human Events, it becomes neceſſary for one People to diſſolve the political Bands which have connected them with another, and to aſſume among the Powers of the Earth, the ſeparate and equal Station to which the Laws of Nature and of Nature's God entitle them, a decent Reſpect to the Opinions of Mankind requires that they ſhould declare the cauſes which impel them to the Separation.

We hold theſe Truths to be ſelf-evident, that all Men are created equal, that they are endowed by their Creator with certain unalienable Rights, that among theſe are Life, Liberty, and the Purſuit of Happineſs—That to ſecure theſe Rights, Governments are inſtituted among Men, deriving their juſt Powers from the Conſent of the Governed, that whenever any Form of Government be-

Ben Franklin owned the *Pennsylvania Gazette* until 1766. The paper continued to be published until 1800.

supply the necessary money. Franklin would supply the talent and hard work.

The print shop did well. People brought their work to Franklin. They knew that he would do a good job. He even printed up paper money for the colony.

In 1729, Ben Franklin also bought a newspaper. He named the paper the

Franklin (left) stands outside his print shop with two friends.

Ben's daughter, Sarah, would later help raise money for American troops during the Revolutionary War.

Pennsylvania Gazette. Before long, his paper earned him money, too.

That same year, Franklin bought out his partner. Now he finally owned his own print shop. Then in 1730, Deborah Read Rogers became his wife.

However, at about the same time, Franklin had a son with another woman. No one knows for sure who the boy's mother was. Some say it was a servant in the Franklin household. In any case, the boy was named William. He lived with the Franklins.

Ben and Deborah Franklin also had two of their own children. Their son, Francis, died of smallpox when he was four. Sometime later, the couple had a daughter named Sarah. Ben nicknamed her Sally.

Deborah and Ben Franklin also opened a store. They sold cloth, soap, tools, and other useful items. Deborah helped with Franklin's printing business too. They were a hardworking and very busy couple.

5 Changing Things for the Better

Ben Franklin was always trying to improve things. That included improving himself. Franklin made a list of good qualities in people. Among these were spending money wisely and treating others fairly.

A FAMOUS BEN FRANKLIN SAYING IS: EARLY TO BED, EARLY TO RISE, MAKES A MAN HEALTHY, WEALTHY, AND WISE.

THAT'S RIGHT! THE SAME IS TRUE FOR DOGS.

Each week Franklin picked a trait from the list. He would try to improve himself in that area. Franklin soon found that this was not easy. Yet he kept trying.

Franklin wished to improve things for others too. In 1731, he and some friends helped start the first public

Franklin helped start the first public library in the American colonies.

This page is from *Poor Richard's Almanack*. It shows an article called "The Art of Making Money." Franklin used pictures as well as words in the article.

library. Then in 1732, Ben Franklin published an almanac called *Poor Richard's Almanack*. **Almanacs** have weather forecasts, recipes, and helpful sayings in them. In Ben Franklin's time, "almanac" was spelled with a "k" on the end of it.

Poor Richard's Almanack was filled was good advice. Many sayings from

Firemen of Franklin's time used a hand pump to spray water on a burning building. They would fill the pump with buckets of water that they got from a well.

This marking was used by Franklin's fire insurance company.

it are still used today. "A penny saved is a penny earned" is just one of these.

Ben Franklin cared deeply about Philadelphia. He wanted the city and its people to do well. So he started a lot of useful community projects.

Franklin worried about fires in the city. People often lost their lives, homes, and businesses in these blazes. In 1736, Franklin began the city's first fire company. He later also helped start a fire insurance company.

In 1736, Ben Franklin was elected clerk of Pennsylvania's **legislature** (government) as well. The following year he was appointed postmaster of Philadelphia. In time, Franklin greatly improved mail service.

But Ben Franklin did not stop there. He wanted to help the sick. So in 1751, he formed a group to start the Pennsylvania Hospital. The hospital is still there today. He also helped found the school that became the University of Pennsylvania.

The Pennsylvania Hospital started by Franklin was located on Pine Street in Philadelphia.

Meanwhile, Ben's newspaper and printing business continued to do well. He set up partnerships with people in other colonies. These businesses did well too.

By 1749, Ben Franklin could afford to retire early. Yet that did not mean that he would do less. Ben was about to become busier than ever.

6 An Inventor and Scientist

Ben Franklin was a very curious person. He liked finding new and better ways to do things. This led to his becoming a respected inventor. Some of his inventions are still used today.

As early as 1743, Franklin designed the Franklin stove. A person could cook on it, but it was used mostly for home heating. The Franklin stove was an improvement over the fireplace. It gave off much more heat while using less fuel.

This is a model of the Franklin stove.

Franklin had always loved to swim. So no one was surprised when he invented swim fins. Swimmers would attach these "fins" to their feet. It helped them swim underwater.

Ben also really enjoyed music. He played the violin, harp, and guitar, as well as other instruments. In 1761, Franklin invented a musical instrument called the glass armonica. Ben used thirty-seven different-sized glass jars to make the armonica. He was quite pleased with his new invention. Ben described its sound as both "sweet" and "heavenly."

Others agreed with him. Ben's armonica became extremely popular. Famous composers wrote music for it.

This glass armonica is on display at the Franklin Institute museum.

The queen of France even paid for glass armonica lessons.

Ben used glass in other ways, too. In 1784, Ben Franklin invented **bifocals**. Bifocals are glasses that have two lenses—one to see up close and one to see farther away.

Franklin had long been interested in science. He studied weather, different rock forms, and fossils. He was also curious about medicine. Franklin looked into the causes of the common cold and other illnesses. He learned a lot about germs and how diseases are spread. Harvard and Yale universities honored Franklin for his work. In London, the Royal Society of Medicine gave him a medal.

These bifocals from the 1700s are much like the ones that Franklin designed.

Very often, Ben Franklin's different interests seemed to be endless. However, it was his work with electricity that helped him become famous. In

In this painting, Franklin performs his famous kite experiment.

Franklin's time, people did not know very much about electricity. They did not understand the force behind lightning. But Franklin believed that lightning was a flow of electricity.

In 1752, he proved this with his well-known kite experiment. Franklin tied a metal key to a kite's string. Then he flew the kite during a thunderstorm.

According to the story, lightning struck the kite. The electrical charge from the lightning traveled down to the key. As a result, Franklin received an electrical shock.

No one knows if the experiment really happened this way. Holding a kite struck by lightning would be extremely dangerous. Franklin could have been killed.

Historians have noted that Ben Franklin usually kept excellent records of his experiments. Yet there is no record of just when this experiment was done. He also did not tell anyone about it for months. Nevertheless, people today believe that the experiment occurred, and Franklin had proved his point. Lightning was electricity.

Ben Franklin continued working with electricity. He often invited his good friends to watch. Once he tried to use electricity to kill a turkey for dinner. He hoped to cook the bird using electricity too. However, Franklin made a terrible mistake. He gave himself the electrical shock instead of the turkey. Franklin was knocked senseless by the jolt. Luckily he was not seriously hurt.

7 A Statesman at Home and Abroad

Ben Franklin always wanted to improve things. As early as 1754, he came up with a plan to unite the colonies. He suggested it at a meeting known as the Albany Congress. So Franklin called it his Albany Plan of Union.

Under this plan, the colonies would unite in order to raise **taxes**. These taxes would be used for defense. The British and French had started fighting in North America. If the British colonies were attacked, Franklin wanted them to be ready and strong.

Franklin used his newspaper to help make his point. He printed the first political cartoon. It was a picture of a snake cut into pieces. The pieces stood for the colonies. Under it were the words: Join or Die.

However, few people liked Franklin's idea. The colonists were not ready to unite. They feared losing control over their own colonies. Great Britain was against the plan, too. It did

Franklin drew this cartoon to try to get the colonists to join together against Britain.

Ben Franklin stands at the left. He asked Britain's government to allow the colonists to collect taxes from some of the King's men.

not want the colonists to become too strong or united. That could threaten the king's power. To Franklin's disappointment, his Albany Plan never took hold. But Franklin still stayed active in politics.

In 1756, Pennsylvania lawmakers sent Franklin to England. He was to ask King George III to solve a problem. Some of the king's men who lived in Britain, but owned land in Pennsylvania, felt they should not have to pay tax for their land in the colony. The colonists wanted their tax dollars. Franklin was to try to settle things in the colonists' favor. And he did so in 1760.

Yet by 1765, the battle over taxing the King's men seemed unimportant. A more serious problem arose in the

King George III of
Great Britain

colonies. Taxes were at the heart of this matter too.

King George III of Britain and **Parliament** (the British form of government) had begun to heavily tax the colonies. The Stamp Tax of 1765 was one of the first taxes. It made the colonists buy government stamps to be placed on newspapers, playing cards, **documents**, and other items. The colonists felt the taxes were unfair. They argued that they had no one to represent them in Parliament.

The colonists refused to give in. They would not pay the taxes. They made threats toward the British tax collectors. The angry colonists also **rebelled** (they disobeyed either through the use of force or breaking the law) in other ways, too. They **boycotted**, or refused, to buy British goods.

While this occurred, Franklin had remained in

BEN FRANKLIN STAYED ON IN ENGLAND HOPING TO SETTLE THINGS BETWEEN THE KING AND THE COLONIES.

IT MUST HAVE BEEN DIFFICULT FOR HIM. WHILE HE WAS GONE, HIS WIFE, DEBORAH, DIED SUDDENLY.

England. He now acted as the colonists' representative. Besides Pennsylvania, Franklin was now also asked to speak for Georgia, New Jersey, and Massachusetts.

Franklin tried to work things out with the king and Parliament. He even spoke before Parliament to explain the colonists' feelings. He also wrote articles and drew cartoons on the subject.

Nevertheless, things worsened. Franklin saw that the king did not care about the colonists. King George III felt that he had a right to tax them. If they rebelled, he would use force against them.

Franklin tried to find a fair way to solve this problem. But the British Parliament did not listen to him. He realized that the situation was hopeless.

Ben Franklin could not help the colonies by remaining in England. He set sail for Philadelphia on March 21, 1775. By the time he had arrived home, war had broken out between Britain and the colonies.

While Franklin was in Britain, American colonists battled British soldiers in Lexington, Massachusetts.

8 A True American

Ben Franklin's ship docked in Philadelphia on April 19, 1775. Things were not going well. His wife had died while he was away. Also, in February, colonial troops had battled the British at Lexington and Concord. Ben had little time to rest. The next morning, he was picked to serve in the Second Continental Congress.

This was a congress made up of representatives from all thirteen colonies. These men had to decide what to do about the trouble with Britain. Things had not improved. The colonists had to prepare for the worst.

Now Franklin also headed Pennsylvania's Committee for Safety. The committee trained the men of Pennsylvania to fight. Later, those men would join together with other colonial soldiers to form the Continental Army.

Ben Franklin was appointed postmaster general as well. He came

The members of the Committees for Safety soon joined together to form the American Continental Army. Now they were ready to fight the British army.

This type of gun, called a musket, was used by the Committees for Safety.

up with new postal routes. The colonies needed to stay in close touch during wartime.

Franklin served on a secret committee, too. This group wrote to important people in Europe. They asked them to side with the colonists.

Ben Franklin felt that the colonies should be independent. So he also served on the committee to write the Declaration of Independence. This was important work. If the colonies voted to break away from Britain, the declaration had to explain why.

Most of this document was written by a young representative from Virginia. His name was Thomas Jefferson. However, Franklin made some important changes to it.

All the changes were approved on July 4, 1776. That day, a new nation was born. All of the thirteen colonies joined to form the new United States of America.

This famous painting by John Trumbull shows the signing of the Declaration of Independence.

9 Fighting for Freedom

The French loved Franklin's cap. It was made from bear fur!

Britain was not about to give up its American colonies. The colonists would have to fight for their freedom. At seventy-one, Ben Franklin was too old to join the army. So he helped in other ways.

First, Franklin was sent to Canada. He asked the Canadians for help in the colonists' fight against Britain. Next, he went to France. Crossing the Atlantic was dangerous. If the British captured his ship, Franklin would surely hang. To the British, Franklin was a **traitor**.

The trip was not easy for Franklin. His health had begun to fail. Yet, he insisted on doing his part.

Though it took some time, Franklin was successful in France. Franklin was a good representative. He made many friends for the new nation. The French also began to believe in the colonists. At the Battle of Saratoga, the

Franklin visited the French king Louis XVI and asked for his country's help.

This is part of the actual Treaty of Paris. Franklin signed his name. His is the third one from the top.

colonists defeated the large well-trained British army. The French were impressed by this victory. They agreed to come to the colonists' aid.

After the colonists defeated Britain, a peace **treaty** was needed. Franklin was one of five men asked to write it. While he was in France, he and several other men worked out the details of the peace treaty. It was called the Treaty of Paris.

Ben Franklin finally left France on May 2, 1785. He had been there for over eight years. During this time, he served as America's ambassador to France. The French were sorry to see him go. Franklin had become quite popular there.

Franklin was also warmly greeted when he returned to the United States. Cannons were fired to welcome him home. People were grateful for all he had done. Ben Franklin had become an American hero.

BEN FRANKLIN WAS SO POPULAR IN FRANCE THAT THE FRENCH PUT HIS PICTURE ON RINGS, HANDKERCHIEFS, AND LOTS OF OTHER THINGS.

IN A LETTER TO HIS DAUGHTER, FRANKLIN SAID—'MY FACE IS AS WELL KNOWN AS THE MOON.'

Heading Home

Ben Franklin was seventy-nine years old when he returned from France. He was not in the best of health. But he knew that his country still needed his help.

A month after his return, Franklin was elected head of Pennsylvania's government. He did his best to help the state. Yet his work did not end there.

Franklin wanted all people to be free. He once owned slaves, but had freed them. Now he hoped to see slavery outlawed. He became president of Pennsylvania's Abolitionist Society. This group also wanted slavery made illegal.

Ben Franklin was also chosen as one of Pennsylvania's **delegates** (representatives) to the Constitutional Convention. These men had a difficult job to do. They would write the U.S. Constitution. This document listed the main laws of the United States.

Now eighty-one, Franklin was the oldest delegate at the Congress. However, he did not have far to travel. The Congress was

Franklin had read about different forms of government. So, he was ready to help with the Constitution.

This statue of Benjamin Franklin is in the Franklin Institute museum in Philadelphia, Pennsylvania.

held in Philadelphia. At the time, it was the largest city in America.

Franklin and the other delegates signed the Constitution on September 17, 1787. These men had done a good job. The U.S. Constitution has lasted for over two hundred years.

Ben Franklin lived to be eighty-four. He died quietly on April 17, 1790. He was given a public funeral. Over twenty thousand people came. In France, a three-day mourning period was declared.

Ben Franklin had been an outstanding American. His ideas were important in shaping our country. He wanted a nation where people lived as equals. Franklin felt that with hard work, anyone should be able to get ahead in the United States of America.

Though he became a famous inventor and scientist, Franklin was much more. Ben Franklin was a man who truly loved his country. He spent much of his time working for the public good. His was a life well lived.

Max and I must be heading home now. We are glad that you spent some time with Ben Franklin and us. Time travel is always more fun with friends. Now, to the time machine!

11 Ben's Good Advice

Ben Franklin was full of good advice. Many of his sayings appeared in *Poor Richard's Almanack*. Others came from letters or speeches. Here are a few of Max's favorites:

Ben Franklin Said . . .	What It Means
An apple a day keeps the doctor away.	Fruits and vegetables are important to a person's health.
A true friend is the best possession.	Nothing is worth more than a very good friend.
Fish and visitors stink after three days.	Guests should know when to leave.
Well done is better than well said.	It is better to do something well than just talk about doing it.
Never leave that till tomorrow which you can do today.	Do not put things off.
Nothing can be said to be certain except death and taxes.	For a person, only dying and paying taxes are sure to happen.
The sleepy fox catches no poultry.	A lazy person gets nowhere.
An ounce of prevention is worth a pound of cure.	It's better to prevent or avoid a problem than have to fix things afterwards.
Three may keep a secret, if two of them are dead.	Don't tell your secrets, if you want to keep them secret.

Farewell Fellow Explorer,

Just wanted to take a moment to tell you a little about the real "Max and me." I am a children's book author and Max is a small, fluffy, white dog. I almost named him Marshmallow because of how he looked. However, he seems to think he's human—so only a more dignified name would do. Max also seems to think that he is a large powerful dog. He fearlessly chases after much larger dogs in the neighborhood. Max was thrilled when the artist for this book drew him as a dog several times his size. He felt that someone in the art world had finally captured his true spirit.

In real life, Max is quite a traveler. I've taken him to nearly every state while doing research for different books. We live in Florida so when we go north I have to pack a sweater for him. When we were in Oregon it rained and I was glad I brought his raincoat. None of this gear is necessary when time traveling. My "take-off" spot is the computer station and as always Max sits faithfully by my side.

Best Wishes,
Elaine & Max
(a small dog with big dreams)

Timeline

1706   Ben Franklin is born on January 17th.

1716   Goes to work in his father's soap and candle shop.

1718   Becomes an apprentice in his brother's print shop.

1723   Runs away to Philadelphia to begin a new life.

1724   Leaves for England.

1726   Returns to Philadelphia from England.

1728   Goes into the printing business with a partner.

1729   Buys a newspaper that he names the *Pennsylvania Gazette*.

1730   Marries Deborah Reed Rogers.

1731   Starts the first public library.

1732   Publishes the first *Poor Richard's Almanack*.

1736   Helps establish Philadelphia's first fire company. That year he is also elected clerk of Pennsylvania's legislature.

1737	Is appointed postmaster.
1743	Invents the Franklin stove.
1748	Retires from the printing business.
1751	Helps establish the Pennsylvania Hospital.
1752	Performs his famous kite experiment.
1762	Invents the glass armonica.
1775	Is a delegate to the Second Continental Congress.
1784	Invents bifocals.
1787	Franklin and the other delegates sign the U.S. Constitution.
1790	Ben Franklin dies on April 17th.

Words to Know

apprentice—A young person who learns a trade by working with a skilled person over a period of time.

christen—To baptize in the Christian faith.

colony—A settlement in a new area.

delegate—A person sent as a representative to an important meeting.

document—A paper containing important information.

historian—A person who studies the past.

legislature—A lawmaking body.

Parliament—A form of government in England in which representatives are elected.

pelt—An animal skin.

tax—Money collected from people to support their government.

traitor—Someone who sides with the enemy of his or her nation.

treaty—An agreement between nations.

Further Reading

Books

Furgang, Kathy. *The Declaration of Independence and Benjamin Franklin of Pennsylvania*. New York: Powerkids Press, 2002.

Giblin, James. *The Amazing Life of Benjamin Franklin*. New York: Scholastic Press, 2000.

Quackenbush, Robert. *The Amazing Life of Benjamin Franklin*. New York: Scholastic Press, 2000.

Schanzer, Rosalyn. *How Ben Franklin Stole the Lightning*. New York: HarperCollins, 2003.

Streissguth, Tom. *Benjamin Franklin*. Minneapolis: Lerner Publications, 2005.

Web Sites

Ben Franklin—An Extraordinary Life. An Electric Mind.

Visit this PBS Web site to learn more about the remarkable civic leader and inventor—Ben Franklin

<http://www.pbs.org/benfranklin/>

Ben's Guide to U.S. Government for Kids—Benjamin Franklin

Learn about Ben Franklin's work as a printer, librarian, inventor, and statesman.

<http://bensguide.gpo.gov/benfranklin/>

Index